The Music Box
A Story of Hope

Story by Tara L. Nielsen
Illustrations by Jeanie

It is only through the dark that one can find light. Only after the storm that one can find strength. And only after one has felt the healing touch of compassion that one can find hope again.
To my sister, with love.
~Tara L. Nielsen

In order for a rose to grow, the soil must first be broken and watered.
To all those who have suffered, who have sought the light within, and to those who suffer: have courage and strength to never give up.
~Jeanie

Copyright © 2016 Tara L. Nielsen

All rights reserved.

No part of this publication may be reproduced, stored, distributed, or transmitted in any form or by any means, including photocopying, recording, electronic or mechanical methods, or otherwise, without the prior written permission of the author, except in the case of brief quotations and certain other noncommercial uses permitted by copyright law.

Printed in the United States of America by IngramSpark

ISBN: 978-0-9973881-1-4

Cover Art and Illustrations done in watercolor by Jeanie
Artwork and Illustrations Copyright © 2016 Jeanie

The Music Box
A Story of Hope

Story by Tara L. Nielsen
Illustrations by Jeanie

There once was a castle, set high upon the tallest mountain, more glorious than any other. The glimmer of gold and silver and the sparkle of precious gems told of the greatest of all who lived there. It glistened in the sunlight, and yet it was simple in structure. It was here that the king lived and watched over all that went on in the world below.

In the hills, below the castle, stood a simple and modest building. When one came near, a certain peace and joy filled his soul, for it was here that the master carver worked and lived. He was a kind, gentle, and loving soul. He made such beautiful treasures that people would make the long journey from the village just to look at them.

Nestled in the valley below the master's shop, on the outskirts of the village, was a thick, majestic forest. Its trees stood noble and strong creating a high leaf canopy. Often the people would come to cut the trees and gather the wood for it was both beautiful and useful.

As the king looked out over all the land, he noticed one tree standing straighter and taller than the others. "What magnificent beauty!" he exclaimed. "Surely this tree will become something wonderful!"

It was not long after that the tree was cut down and taken to a saw mill where it was divided into many boards. Each board wondered what he would become and eagerly waited for someone to purchase him and make him into something beautiful. One board in particular was especially nervous and yet excited as he watched each customer closely, hoping he would soon be chosen.

A man and his son soon purchased several boards. Among them was the one so excited and hopeful. He was so happy to be chosen, he nearly forgot to be nervous. Though anxious to see what he would become, while being carried home, he slipped through the hands of the boy and one end hit hard against the ground. When the father noticed the dents in the board, he sawed off the end letting it fall to the stone floor.

The board knew he was being made into something beautiful and useful and soon forgot the piece of wood that came from him.

The scrap of wood, forgotten on the floor, got kicked from here to there. The cuts and bruises he received hurt, and often, when no one was around, he cried quietly to himself, "I must not be worth anything. There must be no beauty in me at all."

Day after day, as the little scrap tried to stay away from the feet that kicked him about, he watched as the board was made to look grand. Oh, how he wished to be even half as beautiful as the board now was. But he knew he was bruised and deformed, and could never be beautiful.

After the project was completed, he was left in a pile of scraps to be burned. Here he waited until the boy, on his way out to play, stooped down and grabbed him. For one brief moment the little scrap thought there might be something special about him after all.

He soon realized he was wrong as the boy and his friends began playing with him. At first they threw him back and forth. Later they used him like a ball, kicking him hard at the buildings down the alley. They did not seem to care how often he fell or how scratched he became. When they grew tired of their game, they left him all alone in the cold and the rain.

When the rain stopped, a group of smaller children found the scrap of wood. Being too young to carry knives for whittling, they found large stones and began striking and chipping away at him. They soon tired of their game and ran off leaving the little scrap of wood crying to himself in the shadows by the edge of an old building.

About this time the master carver arrived in the village. It was not often that he came down, but when he did it caused great excitement. He traveled down main street looking for items he might use. The villagers were all hopeful that he would purchase something from them, but whether or not he bought anything, he always stopped and talked to everyone he saw.

After loading his wagon, the master carver began the long journey home. As he came around the corner, he noticed a shape in the dark shadow of a building. Stopping, he climbed down to have a closer look. There was the small piece of wood, left all alone to rot. The master carver's heart was full of sorrow, and tears glistened in his eyes as he gently picked up the wood.

At first, the little scrap shook for fear that once again he would be beaten and tossed aside, but he soon felt the gentle stroke of a hand along his rough and battered sides. As the hand touched each bruise and scratch, it would pause slightly, as if trying to sooth him. Eventually the little scrap heard a soft, strong voice. It was a pleasing voice, a sound like running water, and it spoke words of comfort and love to him.

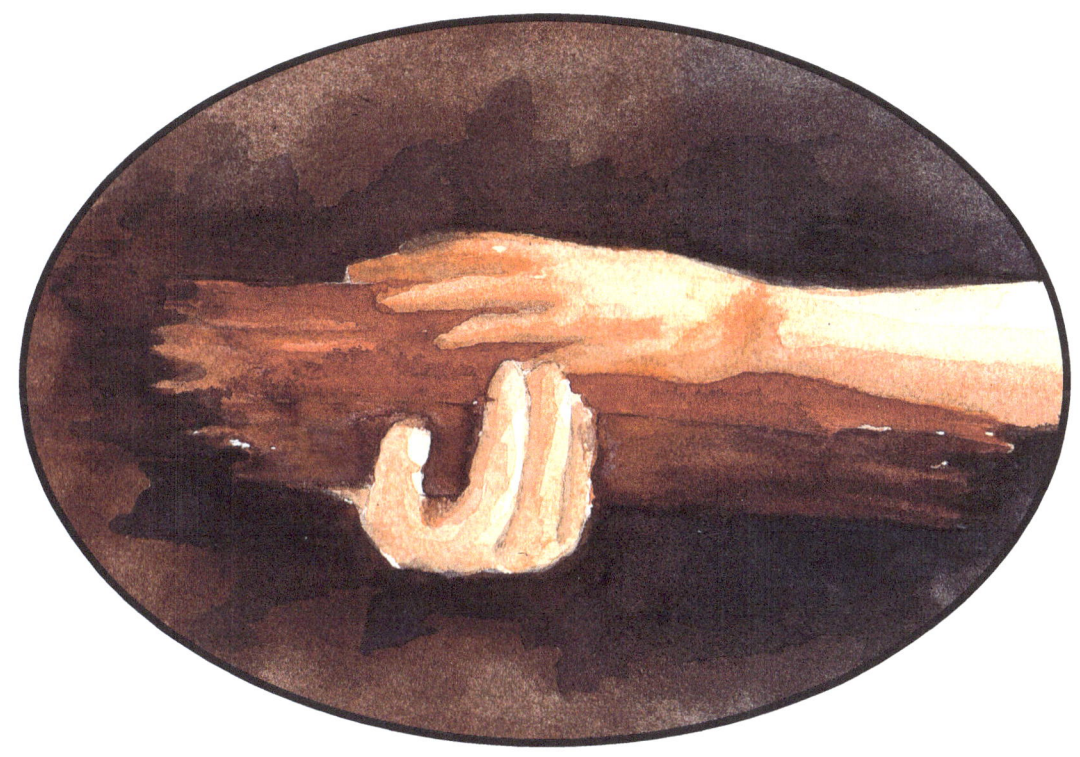

Never before had the little piece of wood encountered such feelings. He was unsure what to make of this new man in whom his fate now rested. Yet something about his voice and touch made the little scrap want to trust him.

And so it was that the little piece of battered wood came to be in the hands of the master carver.

Upon arriving at the carver's home, the little scrap of wood was carried inside. As he looked around, he began to tremble with concern. All around him were beautiful objects. "Surely I do not belong here!" he thought. His heart sank as despair crept over him once again.

The master looked tenderly at the piece of wood. "If you are willing," he said, "I will take away your pain and bring out your true beauty. I will make you into a great treasure. The choice is yours." Then the master carver gently set the little piece of wood upon a sturdy shelf in the center of the room where he could see all around the shop and watch the master at work.

Later that night, as the little scrap pondered all the master carver had said to him, he wondered what the master had meant. "For surely it is not possible to make a great treasure from something so beaten and marked as I am," he thought. Nevertheless, he felt he was safe here, and would not be hurt further, so he resolved to watch the master carver and see what he was able to do.

As the weeks passed, the little scrap watched carefully while the master carver made exquisite gifts. From larger pieces of wood he made beautiful cradles, rocking chairs and fine tables that even the king would be impressed with. From some of the smaller pieces he made sculptures of animals, trains for children, and vases with delicately curved tops. Each piece was more beautiful than the little scrap had ever seen before. Each piece was also unique, special in its own way. Yet they all seemed to belong together as one collection.

Not only did the little scrap watch these creations unfold in the master's hands, but as time went on he saw some pieces leave with the master and never return. The little scrap wondered where these most precious items were taken and why they did not come back, but he could not bring himself to ask.

Eventually the master carver lifted the little wood gently in his hands. "You have seen what I am able to do. Are you ready to let me make you into a great treasure?" he asked.

The little scrap was not sure how to respond. He would love the master carver to make him into something as exquisite as he had the others, but a great sadness hung over him, for he truly had not seen any piece as bruised and battered as he knew he was.

The master carver seemed to understand. "Your bruises and cuts will no longer matter. If you trust me, I will make you into a great treasure, one that will bring great joy to all around you. You must trust me and believe that I am able to take away your hurt and to heal you. If you believe that I can do this, I will make you into a great treasure like the others you have seen."

Inside the little scrap cried, "Yes, yes! Make me into a great treasure. Take away my hurt and heal me!" For never had the little scrap wanted anything more than to be rid of the pain from the life he had before meeting the master.

So the master carver set out to make the little battered wood into something grand.

Again, the little scrap felt the gentleness of the hands of the carver as he examined each broken and damaged area. He held the little piece of wood out away from his face for a better look, deciding exactly what was needed, and what great treasure he would make from him.

As the days passed, the little scrap often found himself in the hands of the carver. Sometimes the carver would chisel away a piece. Other times he would sand the wood. Both hurt. There were times the little scrap thought he could not take another minute of the chipping and scratching, but as the days passed, he noticed the pain less. In its place, he noticed the gentle stroke of the master's hand and the soothing voice as the master spoke to him.

One night, the little scrap reflected on what had happened to him. Looking in the mirror he could see that he was no longer a scrap of unwanted wood, nicked and tattered. Instead, he was a simple rectangle, with a top and a bottom. He was smooth. The marks of neglect were now made beautiful, no longer obvious for what they had once been. He marveled at how those same marks, now healed, helped to make him more attractive. He knew he was far from finished, but he had come to love the feel of the master working with him. The changes he saw were far better than he could ever have imagined he could become. The little scrap of wood was amazed!

After several more weeks, the master carver was finished. He had hollowed out the center of the little box and added a series of metal pieces, which, when fitted together properly, played beautiful music. The top of the wood was now a lid that lifted on hinges, and the outside was intricately painted with vines and roses. The luster of the box was made even greater as the master added a touch of gold and silver which stood out against the glistening reddish brown mahogany. The wood was no longer a "little scrap," but a glorious music box.

When the music box was finished, the master carver placed him on a tiny shelf in the window. Beside the shelf was a rocking chair. It was here that the villagers would sit after making the long journey to listen to the comforting music.

As it happened, a bitter old man, full of many disappointments, came to the shop. He had heard about the music box that brought great joy to all who heard it. Though he would not allow the kindness of others to penetrate his heart, he felt that he must hear the music of this little box.

Upon entering the shop, the master carver glanced up at him. Knowing immediately who the old man was, he motioned to the window where the music box sat. "You may listen for as long as you like," the carver told him and went back to his work.

The old man hesitated only a moment, for something about the box beckoned him near. As he opened the lid, he heard music unlike any other. He immediately thought of his dear wife, who had long since passed away. The music was so peaceful that his heart opened and tears ran freely down his face. It was healing for the man, so he made the trip to the master's shop every day just to listen.

Eventually the old man stopped coming. This made the little box sad, for the old man had become his friend and the little box missed him.

"It was time for him to move on," said the carver. "And so it is for you too."

The little music box did not know what the master meant. He was not sure he wanted to leave the wonderful shop. He loved his special place by the window, and he loved seeing the smiles of the people as they listened to the music the master had so skillfully put inside him. But he had learned to trust the carver and knew this time it was not his choice. He knew the master carver would only do what was best for him.

After carefully wrapping the music box and gently tucking him into his pocket, the master carver left his shop and started into the mountains.

The walk was far, but the music box was warm and comfortable. When they reached the top, and the master carver had taken the little box out of his pocket, he saw before him a great and splendid castle.

"We are here, little music box," said the master carver. "I will present you to the King. He is my father, and all truly great treasures I give to him. He is kind and loving. You will like it here."

With that, the master carried the intricate box into the castle. They came before the king and the master carver gently laid the box on a small stone table. The little music box watched as the master stepped forward and embraced the king.

"I have brought you another great treasure, Father," said the master carver, "One that has brightened the lives of many."

The king turned to look upon the little music box. The music box felt uncertain. He could see that the king's eyes shown with love and patience, yet the little box was not sure he belonged here.

"Is this the little piece of battered wood?" the King inquired softly.

"Yes, Father. He has allowed me to heal him and to make him into an exquisite box, with the music of angels, to sooth the hearts of many. He has shared his music with all around him and has become one of my greatest treasures."

The king looked at the music box once more. "You have done well, little music box. You are truly a great treasure. Come, I have a place for you in my castle, a place of glory where your beauty and gifts will shine forever."

With that, the little music box was gently lifted high onto a shelf where he could look out to all the world below. His lid was opened, never to be shut again, and his music drifted through the hills and into the hearts of all men.

Author Tara L. Nielsen has enjoyed the weight of a pen in her hand ever since she can remember. With a mind full of stories, and a heart full of compassion, Tara's words have touched the hearts of countless individuals. Tara chose to study at the University of Maine at Farmington where she graduated with a B.A. in Psychology. Now a mother of five, and an educator, she spends the majority of her time assisting growing minds and hearts to better understand the world and the people in it. It is her hope that her words will inspire a love of self, an understanding of others, and a desire to overcome the struggles and trials we allow too often to define us.

Born and raised in the beautiful town of Wilton, Maine, Jeanie has sought to express the glorious world in which we all live. A graduate of Brigham Young University - Idaho with a Bachelors in Fine Arts, Jeanie enjoys capturing the stories and emotions of life through her artwork. She seeks to engage viewers and readers in an adventure through their own lives by giving them an aesthetic experience that will help them find gratitude for all they have been blessed with. She wants to encourage all who suffer to lift their heads and follow the light that is radiating around us each and every day. Embrace it, and know that you are not alone; and your beauty is worth more than gold.

A Special Thanks

As it is with most authors, there are too many people who have shared a part of getting me to where I am today to mention everyone by name. I appreciate you all, and wish to give a special thanks to the following:

My husband, Bob, and my children, Gabi, Beth, Jeremy, Peter, and Jacob. Thank you for seeing this through with me. For your enthusiasm, your warm hugs, and your excitement.

My family, near and far, for patience, love and support.

Author Robbin J. Peterson, who insisted I was a "writer" even before I was ready to announce it to the world; who edited and helped me refine this beautiful story, and who pushed me just enough to help me grow.

Author Jennifer C. Petersen, who never let me give up; who always had a word of encouragement.

My father in heaven, for the inspiration and the gift to write.

My teachers, who encouraged and helped me cultivate my talent even from a young age.

My illustrator, Jeanie, who loves this story nearly as much as I do; and who captured the essence of it perfectly.

And the many others who read this story in its rawest forms and insisted it had value, that it helped them, and that they knew someone else who needed it.

Without all of you, this book would not be a reality.

Thank you.

www.ingramcontent.com/pod-product-compliance
Lightning Source LLC
Chambersburg PA
CBHW041128300426
44113CB00003B/94